SWIMMING

by Jason Page

AQUATIC EVENTS

The newly built Sydney International Aquatic Centre is in the heart of the Olympic Park at Homebush Bay. It will be the venue for most of the 44 aquatic events.

COOL!

The first modern Olympic swimming event was the 100-meter freestyle, held in 1896. There were only three competitors, and the race was held not in a swimming pool but in the the icy cold waters of the Bay of Zea, off the coast of Greece. Competitors simply dived off a boat and swam to the shore! The race was won by a 19-year-old Hungarian sailor named Alfred Hajos.

SUPER STATS

There will be 1,150 athletes taking part in the aquatic events at the Sydney Olympics. All together, they would fill two jumbo jets!

FOUR OF THE BEST

Swimming events were not held at the ancient Olympic Games, but they have been included in every modern Olympics. The proper name of the sport is "aquatics," and it's made up of four separate disciplines: swimming, diving, water polo, and synchronized swimming.

NEW FOR SYDNEY

Several new events will make their Olympic debut at the 2000 Games in Sydney, including synchronized diving, shown here, and women's water polo.

OLYMPICS FACT FILE

The Olympic Games were first held in Olympia, Greece, about 3,000 years ago. They took place every four years until they were abolished in A.D. 393.

A Frenchman named Pierre de Coubertin (1863–1937) revived the Games, and the first modern Olympics were held in Athens in 1896.

The modern Games have been held every four years since 1896, except in 1916, 1940, and 1944, because of war. Special 10th-anniversary Games took place in 1906.

The symbol of the Olympic Games is five interlocking colored rings. Together, they represent the five different continents from which athletes come to compete.

GOLDEN GREATS

Mark Spitz

Mark Spitz (USA) is the greatest swimmer ever seen at the Olympic Games. Between 1968 and 1972, he won a total of nine golds, a silver, and a bronze. His record tally of seven victories at one Olympics is unmatched in any sport to this day!

50-METER FREESTYLE

The 50-meter freestyle covers just one length of the pool, making it the shortest of all the swimming races—and the fastest.

THE NAME'S BIONDI...

In 1988, the men's 50-meter freestyle was won by Matt Biondi (USA), the only swimmer who has managed to win as many Olympic medals as Mark Spitz! Between 1984 and 1992, Biondi swam away with eight golds, two silvers, and a bronze.

Amy Van Dyken

ANIMAL OLYMPIANS

The gold medal for sprint swimming in the animal kingdom goes to the mighty sailfish. With a top speed of 68 mph (110 km/h) this super-fast fish would finish the 50-meter freestyle in just 1.6 seconds!

TOUGH COMPETITION

Amy Van Dyken (USA) is the reigning Olympic champion in the women's 50-meter freestyle. But winning the gold at the 1996 Games in Atlanta wasn't easy. She had to beat Jingyi Le (CHN), the fastest female swimmer the world has ever seen.

DID YOU KNOW?

An Olympic 50-meter freestyle champion swims at a top speed of 5 mph (8 km/h)—that's twice as fast as a normal walking pace.

An Olympic swimming pool is 6 feet (1.8 meters) deep—that's deep enough to go over the head of an average adult.

The 50-meter event (or 50 yards as it was then known) first appeared at the Olympic Games in 1904. It was not held again until 1988—84 years later.

LEARN TO CRAWL

In freestyle races, any stroke can be used — but swimmers always choose the front crawl because it's the fastest stroke. In the front crawl, one arm goes over the swimmer's head while the other is pushed down through the water. At the same time, the swimmer kicks his or her legs quickly up and down—up to six kicks per arm stroke.

Alexander Popov

POPOV'S PLANS

Alexander Popov (RUS) won both the 50- and 100-meter freestyles at the last two Olympic Games. He's going for another golden double at Sydney! If Popov succeeds, he'll set a record of three consecutive golds in two events.

WOMEN'S RECORDS: WORLD: Jingyi Le (CHN) 24.51 sec. **OLYMPIC**: Wenyi Yang (CHN) 24.79 sec.

Even short hair creates water resistance and slows swimmers down. That's why most swimmers wear swimming caps.

Goggles protect a swimmer's eyes from harmful chemicals in the water.

Swimming costumes are made of light, flexible materials, including Teflon—also used to make nonstick frying pans!

DID YOU KNOW?

The 1984 women's 100-meter freestyle final was a dead heat. Both swimmers were awarded gold medals.

The swimming events at the 1900 Olympics included a 200-meter obstacle race!

Women competed in swimming events at the Olympics for the first time in 1912.

Streamlined swimming

MEN'S RECORDS: WORLD: 100 meters: Alexander Popov (RUS) 48.21 sec. **200 meters:** Ian Thorpe (AUS) 1 min. 46 sec.
OLYMPIC: 100 meters: Matt Biondi (USA) 48.63 sec. **200 meters:** Yvegeniy Sadovyi (EUN) 1 min. 46.7 sec.

SHORT-DISTANCE FREESTYLE

The 100-meter and 200-meter races give swimmers a chance to demonstrate speed over a longer distance.

A NEW DAWN?

Dawn Fraser (AUS) won the women's 100-meter freestyle in 1956, 1960, and 1964. She was the first swimmer ever to win an Olympic gold in the same event three times in a row.

Dawn Fraser

SPLIT-SECOND TIMING

Swimming races are timed electronically. The signal to start the race automatically starts the clock. As each swimmer touches the wall at the end of the race, a pressure pad records his or her time to within one hundredth of a second!

GET OUT OF MY WAY!

In 1920, the final of the men's 100-meter freestyle had to be raced again after an Australian competitor complained that a U. S. swimmer had impeded him. However, it made no difference to the result. Both races were won by Duke Kahanamoku—a member of the Hawaiian Royal Family.

SUPER STATS

The pool used at the Olympic Games is 55 yards (50 meters) long—almost double the length of two tennis courts placed end to end.

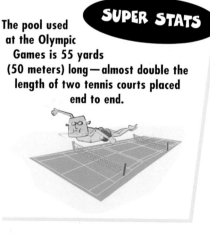

WOMEN'S RECORDS: WORLD: 100 meters: Jingyi Le (CHN) 54.01 sec. **200 meters:** Franziska van Almsick (GER) 1 min. 56.78 sec.
OLYMPIC: 100 meters: Jingyi Le (CHN) 54.5 sec. **200 meters:** Heike Friedrich (GDR) 1 min. 57.65 sec.

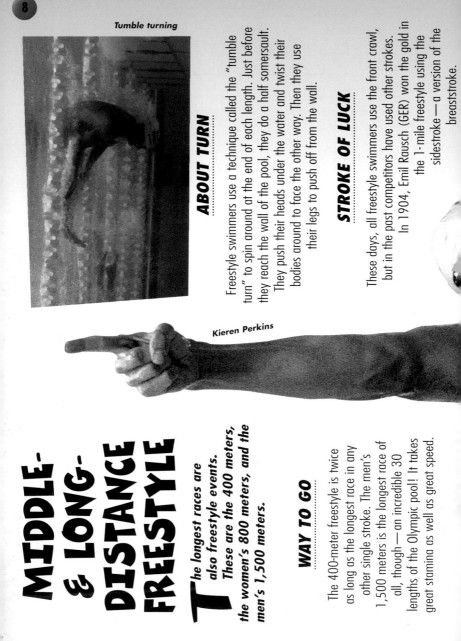

Tumble turning

ABOUT TURN

Freestyle swimmers use a technique called the "tumble turn" to spin around at the end of each length. Just before they reach the wall of the pool, they do a half somersault. They push their heads under the water and twist their bodies around to face the other way. Then they use their legs to push off from the wall.

STROKE OF LUCK

These days, all freestyle swimmers use the front crawl, but in the past competitors have used other strokes. In 1904, Emil Rausch (GER) won the gold in the 1-mile freestyle using the sidestroke—a version of the breaststroke.

Kieren Perkins

MIDDLE- & LONG-DISTANCE FREESTYLE

The longest races are also freestyle events. These are the 400 meters, the women's 800 meters, and the men's 1,500 meters.

WAY TO GO

The 400-meter freestyle is twice as long as the longest race in any other single stroke. The men's 1,500 meters is the longest race of all, though—an incredible 30 lengths of the Olympic pool! It takes great stamina as well as great speed.

MEN'S RECORDS: WORLD: 400 meters: Ian Thorpe (AUS) 3 min. 41.83 sec. **1,500 meters:** Kieren Perkins (AUS) 14 min. 41.66 sec.
OLYMPIC: 400 meters: Yvegeniy Sadovyi (EUN) 3 min. 45 sec. **1,500 meters:** Kieren Perkins (AUS) 14 min. 43.48 sec.

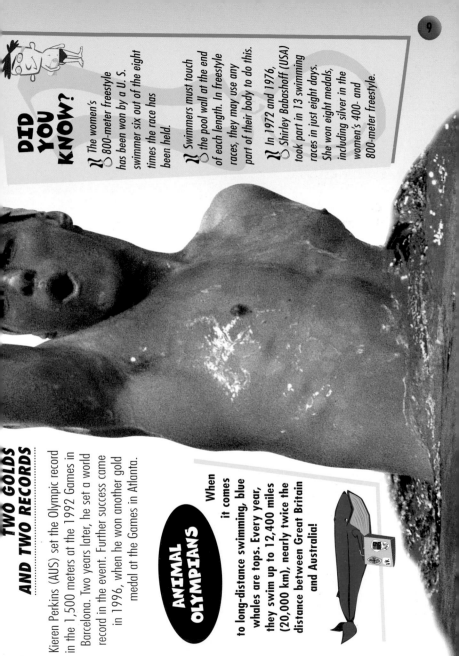

DID YOU KNOW?

♔ The women's 800-meter freestyle has been won by a U. S. swimmer six out of the eight times the race has been held.

♔ Swimmers must touch the pool wall at the end of each length. In freestyle races, they may use any part of their body to do this.

♔ In 1972 and 1976, Shirley Babashoff (USA) took part in 13 swimming races in just eight days. She won eight medals, including silver in the women's 400- and 800-meter freestyle.

TWO GOLDS AND TWO RECORDS

Kieren Perkins (AUS) set the Olympic record in the 1,500 meters at the 1992 Games in Barcelona. Two years later, he set a world record in the event. Further success came in 1996, when he won another gold medal at the Games in Atlanta.

ANIMAL OLYMPIANS

When it comes to long-distance swimming, blue whales are tops. Every year, they swim up to 12,400 miles (20,000 km), nearly twice the distance between Great Britain and Australia!

WOMEN'S RECORDS: WORLD: **400 meters**: Janet Evans (USA) 4 min. 3.85 sec. **800 meters**: Janet Evans (USA) 8 min. 16.22 sec.
OLYMPIC: **400 meters**: Janet Evans (USA) 4 min. 3.85 sec. **800 meters**: Janet Evans (USA) 8 min. 20.2 sec.

BREASTSTROKE

Competitors in the 100- and 200-meter breaststroke are always looking for loopholes in the rules that will help them swim faster. But the breaststroke has more regulations than any other stroke.

HANDY ADVICE

Breaststroke swimmers must touch the side of the pool with both hands at the end of every length. Failure to do so means instant disqualification!

SUPER STATS

The breaststroke is the slowest stroke. The fastest breaststroke champion has a top speed of just 3.7 mph (6 km/h). You could run about three times as fast.

HEAD UP

About 30 years ago, breaststroke swimmers discovered they could swim faster underwater. So a rule was introduced that says their heads must break the surface on every stroke — except at the start of the race or when turning. Here's Frédéric Deburghgraeve (BEL), the reigning 100-meter Olympic champion and world record holder, showing how it's done!

Frédéric Deburghgraeve

MEN'S RECORDS: **WORLD**: **100 meters**: Frédéric Deburghgraeve (BEL) 1 min. 0.6 sec. **200 meters**: Mike Barrowman (USA) 2 min. 10.16 sec.
OLYMPIC: **100 meters**: Frédéric Deburghgraeve (BEL) 1 min. 0.6 sec. **200 meters**: Mike Barrowman (USA) 2 min. 10.16 sec.

Racing dives

WHAT A DIVE!

All swimming races (apart from backstroke events) start with the competitors diving off the starting blocks and into the pool. A good racing dive is shallow and powerful. Breaststroke swimmers often dive slightly deeper than competitors in other strokes as they are allowed to swim their first stroke underwater.

DID YOU KNOW?

♪ Swimming races are started with just two commands: "Take your marks" and "Go."

♪ In 1936, the bronze medal in the women's 200-meter breaststroke was won by Inge Sörensen (DEN). She was only 12 years old at the time!

♪ If the men's 100-meter freestyle champion had a race with the 100-meter breaststroke champ, the freestylist would win by more than 10 seconds!

BREAST EFFORT

In the breaststroke, the swimmer's arms and legs stay underwater. Both arms move together in a circular motion, stretching out in front of the swimmer, then pushing down through the water and coming back underneath the chin. At the same time, the swimmer kicks his or her legs like a frog.

WOMEN'S RECORDS: WORLD: 100 meters: Penelope Heyns (RSA) 1 min. 6.52 sec. **200 meters:** Penelope Heyns (RSA) 2 min. 23.64 sec.
OLYMPIC: 100 meters: Penelope Heyns (RSA) 1 min. 7.02 sec. **200 meters:** Penelope Heyns (RSA) 2 min. 25.41 sec.

FLYING THE FLAG

Backstroke swimmers can't actually see where they are going! A row of flags is hung across the pool, 5 meters from each end, to warn them they are getting close to the pool wall. When turning, swimmers can use any part of their body to touch the wall.

DID YOU KNOW?

?) An Olympic swimming lane is 8 feet (2.5 meters) wide.

?) The fastest swimmers go in the middle lanes; the slower ones get the outside lanes.

?) Floating lane dividers keep swimmers from bumping into each other and reduce the waves swimmers create.

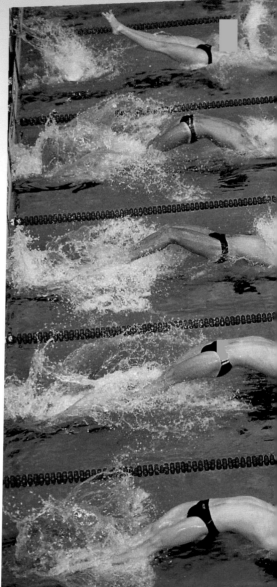

Starting a backstroke race

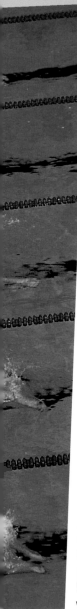

BACKSTROKE

The key to success in the 100- and 200-meter backstroke is to keep your body as straight as possible.

RECORD COLLECTION

Dawn Fraser isn't the only swimmer to hold three Olympic golds in one event. Kristina Egerszegi (HUN) won the 200-meter backstroke event three times between 1988 and 1996 and holds five golds in all. At the 1992 Games in Barcelona, she also set two Olympic records when she won both the 100 meters and 200 meters.

Kristina Egerszegi

CRAWLING BACK

In the backstroke (or back crawl), swimmers must remain on their backs at all times except when turning. The leg action is the same as in the front crawl. The arms move one at a time in a circle over the swimmer's head and through the water.

WET START

Instead of diving off the starting blocks, backstroke swimmers hold on to a rail along the edge of the pool and lean back with their knees bent and their feet against the wall. When they hear the starting pistol, they launch themselves backward by pushing off the wall with their feet.

ANIMAL OLYMPIANS

Sea otters often swim on their backs, too. In fact, they can even do it in their sleep!

BUTTERFLY

The butterfly is the newest Olympic stroke. The 100-meter event was introduced in 1956 for women and 1968 for men; the 200 meters was held for the first time in 1968 for women and 1956 for men!

ANIMAL OLYMPIANS

The massive manta ray is the butterfly champion at the Animal Olympics. It swims by beating its giant fins like underwater wings. Its fins can measure more than 20 feet (6 meters) across, tip to tip.

BALANCING ACT

Swimmers need to be very strong, especially in butterfly events. However, if the swimmer's muscles are too big, the swimmer is unable to move smoothly and his or her swimming technique is affected. An Olympic swimmer needs to be supple, too.

Susan O'Neill

Denis Pankratov

Denis Pankratov (RUS) won the gold in both men's butterfly events at the last Games.

FLOAT LIKE A BUTTERFLY

The butterfly is the hardest stroke to master. Swimmers swing both their arms through the air then pull them down through the water. At the same time, they move their legs in a "dolphin kick," keeping their feet together while moving them up and down.

Susan O'Neill (AUS) is the reigning Olympic champion in the women's 200-meter butterfly. She won a bronze medal in the event at the Olympics in 1992 and will be aiming for her third medal in a row when she competes at Sydney.

DID YOU KNOW?

Although almost all butterfly swimmers use the dolphin kick, they may also use the breaststroke kick.

The 200-meter butterfly world record held by Mary Meagher (USA) is 19 years old—the oldest world record ever.

Kristin Otto became the only person ever to win gold medals in three different strokes when she won the women's 100-meter butterfly, backstroke, and freestyle in 1988.

WOMEN'S RECORDS: WORLD: 100 meters: Jenny Thompson (USA) 57.88 sec. **200 meters:** Mary Meagher (USA) 2 min. 5.96 sec. **OLYMPIC: 100 meters:** Hong Quian (CHN) 58.62 sec. **200 meters:** Mary Meagher (USA) 2 min. 6.9 sec.

Tom Dolan

A RECORD RECORD

Olympic gold medalist Tom Dolan (USA) broke the world record in the men's 400-meter medley in 1994. The Olympic record was set in 1992. However, the Olympic record in the women's event has stood for 20 years — longer than any other current swimming record.

DID YOU KNOW?

ⁿ Tamas Darnyi (HUN) is the only person to have won both the 200-meter and 400-meter medley events at two Olympic Games. He also holds the 400-meter medley Olympic record.

ⁿ An indoor pool was first used at the Olympics in 1948. Until then, races had been held outside.

ⁿ Competitors can be disqualified if the judges think that their swimsuits are too skimpy!

FOUR-STROKE POWER

The medley is a four-stroke race. Competitors must use a different stroke to swim each quarter of the race, in this order: first, the butterfly; second, the backstroke; third, the breaststroke, and finally, the freestyle.

CHILL OUT

According to Olympic regulations, the temperature of the water in the pool should be between 77°F and 81°F (25°C and 27°C), which is slightly cooler than most public swimming pools.

MEN'S RECORDS: WORLD: **200 meters**: Jani Sievinen (FIN) 1 min. 58.16 sec. **400 meters**: Tom Dolan (USA) 4 min. 12.3 sec.
OLYMPIC: **200 meters**: Attila Czene (HUN) 1 min. 59.91 sec. **400 meters**: Tamas Darnyi (HUN) 4 min. 14.23 sec.

MEDLEY

Each competitor must use all four different strokes in the 200- and 400-meter individual medleys.

CLOSE ENCOUNTER

The narrowest victory in Olympic history occurred in 1972, in the final of the men's 400-meter medley. Gunnar Larsson (SWE) beat Tim McKee (USA) by just two thousandths of a second — a distance of 3 mm!

SUPER STATS

BANNED!

At the 1996 Games, Michelle Smith (IRL) won gold medals in the 200-meter and 400-meter individual relays, plus a gold in the 400-meter freestyle and a bronze in the 200-meter butterfly. However, her glory at the Olympics soon turned to disgrace when she failed a drug test and was banned from taking part in future competitions.

Michelle Smith

The current Olympic records in both the men's and the women's 400-meter individual medleys are more than 30 seconds faster than the winning times when the races were first held in 1964 — that's long enough to do another length!

WOMEN'S RECORDS: WORLD: 200 meters: Yanyan Wu (CHN) 2 min. 9.72 sec. **400 meters:** Yan Chen (CHN) 4 min. 34.79 sec. **OLYMPIC: 200 meters:** Lin li (CHN) 2 min. 11.65 sec. **400 meters:** Petra Schneider (GDR) 4 min. 36.29 sec.

RELAY

Teams of four swimmers each swim a quarter of the race in the 4 x 100-meter freestyle, 4 x 200-meter freestyle, and 4 x 100-meter medley relays.

CLEAN SWEEP

The United States has always dominated the relays. At the 1996 Olympics in Atlanta, U. S. swimmers won every one of the six races. The U. S. women's 4 x 100-meter freestyle team (seen here celebrating its victory) also set an Olympic record, as did the women's 4 x 200-meter team.

SUPER STATS

There have been 68 relay races held at the Olympics. The United States has won 49 of them!

MEDLEY MIX

In the medley relay, each member of the team uses a different stroke. The first swimmer swims with the backstroke, the second with the breaststroke, the third with the butterfly, and the fourth swims freestyle.

MEN'S RECORDS: WORLD: 4 x 100-meters fr.: United States 3 min. 15.11 sec. **4 x 200-meters fr.:** Australia 7 min. 8.79 sec. **4 x 100-meters m.r.:** United States 3 min. 34.84 sec.
OLYMPIC: 4 x 100-meters fr.: United States 3 min. 15.41 sec. **4 x 200-meters fr.:** Unified Team 7 min. 11.95 sec. **4 x 100-meters m.r.:** United States 3 min. 34.84 sec.

GO APE, MAN

The 800-meter freestyle relays in 1924 and 1928 were won by the team from the United States. One of the members of that team was Johnny Weissmuller, the greatest swimmer of his day. He won a total of five Olympic golds and eventually went on to become a movie star — by playing Tarzan in Hollywood movies!

Johnny Weissmuller as Tarzan

U. S. women's 4 x 100-meter freestyle team

DID YOU KNOW?

The U. S. teams have won the men's 4 x 100-meter freestyle every time the event has been held at the Games!

Eleanor Holm (USA), who won the 100-meter backstroke in 1932, starred as Tarzan's girlfriend, Jane, in a film made in 1938.

The oldest person to win a medal in any swimming event was 46-year-old William Henry (GBR), who won a bronze in the 1906 freestyle relay.

WAIT FOR IT!

During relay races, each swimmer must wait for his or her teammate to touch the wall before diving in. If a swimmer starts too soon, the whole team is disqualified.

WOMEN'S RECORDS: WORLD: 4 x 100-meters fr.: China 3 min. 37.91 sec. 4 x 200-meters fr.: German Democratic Republic 7 min. 55.47 sec. 4 x 100-meters m.r.: China 4 min. 1.67 sec.
OLYMPIC: 4 x 100-meters fr.: United States 3 min. 39.29 sec. 4 x 200-meters fr.: United States 7 min. 59.87 sec. 4 x 100-meters m.r.: United States 4 min. 2.54 sec.

DIVING

Diving has been part of the Olympics since 1904. The Games at Sydney will introduce two new synchronized diving events.

TAKE FIVE

There are five basic types of dives, known as forward, backward, reverse, inward, and twist. However, there are more than 100 recognized variations. Divers try to impress the judges by performing gymnastic moves, such as somersaults, tucks, and pikes, in midair.

Jenny Keim and Kathy Pesek (USA)

Greg Louganis

IT'S A SYNCH

Synchronized diving, in which two divers perform together, will be held for the first time at the Games in Sydney. The idea is that divers should mirror one another as closely as possible, and they are judged as a pair. There will be both springboard and platform synchro competitions.

There is no such thing as a world or Olympic record for diving.

DID YOU KNOW?

♔ Diving was invented by Swedish and German gymnasts around 300 years ago as a way of practicing their moves.

♔ A diver's body should be perfectly straight as he or she enters the water — the smaller the splash, the better the dive!

♔ Greg Louganis is the most successful Olympic diver ever; he won both the springboard and the platform events in 1984 and 1988 and a silver in the platform in 1976.

OUCH!

While attempting a reverse dive at the 1988 Olympics, Greg Louganis (USA) hit his head on the springboard and was badly injured. However, he refused to pull out of the competition and, with his head still in bandages, went on to win his fourth Olympic gold medal!

SPRING INTO ACTION

Olympic diving competitions include both springboard and platform events.

The springboard is just 3 meters above the pool and is very flexible. By jumping on it, competitors can spring high into the air. You can find out about platform diving on pages 22–23.

ANIMAL OLYMPIANS

At the Animal Olympics, the sperm whale would win the diving by a mile — or a mile-and-a-half (2.4 km) to be exact. That's how deep these huge creatures can dive in search of something to eat.

DIVING
(CONTINUED)

The platform dive takes strength, courage, and balance.

Dimitri Sautin

NEED A HAND?

Here the reigning Olympic platform champion, Dimitri Sautin (RUS), is shown performing an armstand dive, which is only done from the platform. Competitors start by doing a handstand at the very edge of the board, then push off with their arms.

GOLDEN AGE

The reigning women's champion in both the platform and springboard diving events is Mingxia Fu (CHN). In 1990, she became the youngest world diving champion — at the age of 11! Since then, the rules have changed. All divers in both world and Olympic competitions must be at least 14 years old.

ANIMAL OLYMPIANS

As platform divers hit the water, they are falling through the air at up to 34 mph (55 km/h). When peregrine falcons dive down on their unsuspecting prey, they reach speeds of around 217 mph (350 km/h).

10-meter platform board

7.5-meter platform boards (not used in Olympic competitions)

5-meter platform boards (not used in Olympic competitions)

3-meter springboards

A jet of water causes tiny ripples on the surface of the pool underneath the diving boards. Without it, the divers would not be able to see where the water began.

JUDGE & JURY

The individual diving events are judged by a panel of seven judges. Nine judges score the synchronized dives. The number of points per dive is awarded as follows: first, the judges mark each dive out of 10 for performance; then they multiply their scores by a number according to the difficulty of the dive — the harder the dive, the higher the number.

DID YOU KNOW?

§ Klaus Dibiasi (ITA) won the platform competition in 1968, 1972, and 1976 — the only Olympic diver to have won the same event three times in a row.

§ The platform dive is also known as the high board — for obvious reasons!

§ The first Olympic diving competition for women was held in 1912.

GAME ON

Each water polo match consists of four 7-minute bouts. There are two referees to ensure fair play. The pool must be 30 meters long, 20 meters wide, and at least 1.8 meters deep. The court is marked with lines painted on the bottom of the pool.

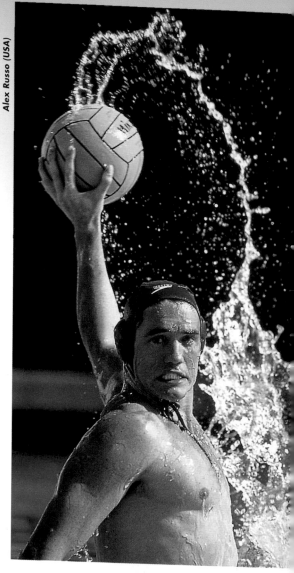

Alex Russo (USA)

DID YOU KNOW?

The first Olympic water polo tournament was won by the Osborne Swimming Club from Manchester, representing Great Britain.

A member of the winning Hungarian team in 1932 and 1936 had only one leg.

In 1968, the team from the German Democratic Republic beat its opponents from the United Arab Emirates 19–2 — a record score!

TOUGH PLAY

To play water polo, competitors need the stamina of a long-distance swimmer, the accuracy of a soccer player, and the strength of a wrestler.

WATER POLO

Water polo was first played at the Olympics in 1900. It was the only team sport at the early Games apart from soccer.

POLO CRAZY

Water polo is a bit like an aquatic version of soccer. Each side has seven players, and the idea is to score as many points as

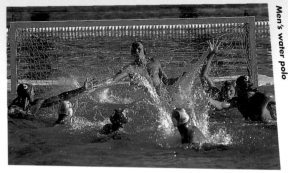

Men's water polo

possible by throwing the ball into the opposition's goal. Players may only use one hand when passing or shooting, and no one except the goalkeeper is allowed to touch the bottom or sides of the pool.

Hungary has won the Olympic water polo tournament more times than any other country, with six victories to its credit. Great Britain is second with four wins (even though it hasn't won since 1920), while Italy and Yugoslavia share third place with three wins each.

SUPER STATS

HUNGARY	~~IIII~~ I
GREAT BRITAIN	IIII
ITALY	III
YUGOSLAVIA	III

MAD HATTERS

Players wear colored caps to show which side they are on. Usually one team wears white and the other blue. Goalkeepers usually wear red caps. The caps have ear protectors and chin straps to keep them from being pulled off.

The ball is the same size as a soccer ball.

WATER POLO
(CONTINUED)

Until now, water polo has been a men-only sport at the Games, but women's teams will be able to compete for the first time at the Sydney Olympics.

ONES TO WATCH

Who will become the first female Olympic water polo champions? Both the Dutch and the Italian teams are strong contenders, but the Australian women's team also has a good chance of winning the gold — and they will have the home crowd cheering them all the way!

SUPER STATS

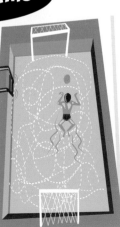

Water polo players can often swim up to 3 miles (5 km) during a match.

BLOCK TACTICS

When defending, players try to block the other team's shots using their arms and body. By kicking furiously with their legs (remember, they are not allowed to touch the bottom of the pool), they try to leap out of the water in front of the attacker just as he or she throws the ball. It takes great strength — and great timing!

GET OUT OF THE POOL

Water polo is a rough, physical sport, but players are not allowed to dunk or hold on to each other. Fouls can result in players being sent out of the pool for 45 seconds; three such offenses usually means they stay out for the rest of the match!

FREE THROWS

As in soccer, if the ball goes out of play (in this case, if it lands outside the pool) the team that touched it last is penalized, and the other team is given a throw-in. Free throws are also awarded in the event of a foul. If a serious offense is committed by one side, its opponents are given a free shot just 13 feet (4 meters) from the goal.

Maureen O'Toole (USA) and Gillian Vanden Berg (NED)

DID YOU KNOW?

Water polo players are not allowed to wear goggles.

In addition to the two referees, there are several other officials whose job it is to watch out for fouls.

Each team is allowed to make four substitutions during a match.

WATER MUSIC

Speakers in the wall of the pool enable the competitors to hear the music while they are underwater. This makes it possible for swimmers to move together with split-second timing.

DID YOU KNOW?

♫ The synchro duet was held in 1984 and 1992 but not at the 1996 Olympics.

♫ In 1992, the winners of both the gold and the silver medals were twins: Karen and Sarah Josephson (USA) won the gold, and Penny and Vicky Vilagos (CAN) won the silver.

♫ Japan has taken third in the duet event in every Olympic final!

Olga Brousnikina

TWO OLGAS

All the gold medals in synchro events have been won by either Canada or the United States. But that looks set to change in Sydney! Olga Brousnikina (right) and Olga Sedakova (RUS) are the reigning world champions and hot favorites to win the duet event.

SYNCHRO DUET

Synchronized swimming appeared as an exhibition event at the Olympics from 1948 to 1968, before becoming a full medal sport in 1984.

BEAUTY TIPS

Competitors use waterproof lipstick and makeup to help them look their best. Instead of wearing a swimming cap, some swimmers put gelatin in their hair. This means their hair stays perfectly in place, even underwater!

SHALL WE DANCE?

Synchro began in Canada in the 1920s and was originally called water ballet. Like ballet, it involves moving to music but instead of dancing, competitors perform in water. Only women are allowed to compete in synchro, which makes it the only swimming discipline with no men's event.

SUPER STATS

There are almost 200 different recognized moves in synchronized swimming. So if you practiced four moves a week, it would take you almost a whole year to learn them all.

REIGNING OLYMPIC CHAMPIONS: United States.

SYNCHRO TEAM

The team competition was introduced for the first time at the 1996 Olympics. Each team is made up of eight swimmers.

PART ONE...

Both the duet and the team events are made up of two parts. The first is a technical routine in which competitors must perform specific moves in a certain order and within a set time.

...AND PART TWO!

The second part of the competition is a free routine without restrictions. This gives the swimmers a chance to show off their skills with as much imagination as possible.

synchro team from the Netherlands

ANIMAL OLYMPIANS

Herrings are the synchro swimming champions of the animal kingdom. They swim together in huge groups (called schools) sometimes comprising several million fish, with each one following almost exactly the movements of the rest.

Each country may enter just one team and one pair.

WINNING BY A NOSE (CLIP)

A nose clip is the most essential piece of equipment that synchro swimmers need. It prevents water from entering their nose, helping them to hold their breath and stay submerged longer. Competitors are also allowed to wear a swimming cap and goggles if they wish.

Synchronized swimmer

MAKING YOUR POINT

Two panels of five judges award points for each part of the competition. One panel scores the execution of the moves—how well they are performed. The other panel scores the overall performance—how beautifully the different moves are linked together.

DID YOU KNOW?

In the 1940s, a number of synchro swimming musical shows were produced involving hundreds of swimmers; some were even made into Hollywood films!

Boosts, rockets, thrusts, and twirls are all names for different synchro moves.

Until 1992, there was also a solo synchro competition for individual medalists.

Competitors select their own music.

INDEX

Acknowledgments

We would like to thank Ian Hodge, Rosalind Beckman, Jackie Gaff and Elizabeth Wiggans for their assistance. Cartoons by John Alston.

Copyright © 2000 *ticktock* Publishing Ltd. Printed in Hong Kong.

First published in Great Britain by ticktock Publishing Ltd., The Offices in the Square, Hadlow, Tonbridge, Kent TN11 0DD, Great Britain.
Picture Credits: Allsport: IFC, OFC, 2–3t, 3b, 4–5t, 5b, 6–7 (main pic), 7tr, 8tr, 8–9c, 10–11t, 10–11b, 12–13 (main pic), 13tr, 14–15b, 15t, 16–17t, 16–17b, 18–19c, 20tl, 20–21 (main pic), 22l, 22–23t, 24–25 (main pic), 25t, 26–27t, 26–27b, 28–29t, 28–29b, 30–31c, 31tr; Ronald Grant Archive: 19tr. Picture research by Image Select.

Library of Congress Cataloging-in-Publication Data

Page, Jason.
  Swimming : sprints, medleys, diving, water polo, and lots, lots more / by Jason Page.
    p. cm. -- (Zeke's Olympic pocket guide)
Includes index.
Summary: Describes the aquatic events of the Olympic Games and previews the athletic competition at the 2000 Summer Olympics in Sydney, Australia.
  ISBN 0-8225-5056-3 (pbk. : alk. paper)
  1. Swimming--Juvenile literature. 2. Olympics--Juvenile literature. [1. Swimming. 2. Olympics.] I. Title. II. Series.
  GV837.6 .P24 2000
  797.21--dc21

00-008100